I AM MORE
— *than* —
ENOUGH

3 Ways to Overcome the Fear
Your Own Reflection

Ahmard Moore Vital

Ahmard Vital

Cover Layout Designed by Mohamed Musthafa
Cover Photography by Chrissy Johnson, Steve Halama

Edited by Sharon Mignerey

For additional copies of this book:
Contact – info@ahmardvital.com

For Booking, Media Inquiries: info@ahmardvital.com

Printed in the United States of America

DEDICATION

To my fathers, Harry and Melvin, whose last names I bear. Thank you both for giving me the foundation for this journey called life.

CONTENTS

Introduction
Good From the Start...............…..………..1

Chapter 1
Image is Everything ……………….…..7

Chapter 2
Accepting Yourself…………………...15

Chapter 3
Mindful Changes………………………..25

Chapter 4
I AM-Ness: Time to Activate………...33

Chapter 5
Poem – Listen ……………….....……….36

Vital Thoughts – The Finale………...39

Contact Us ……………………………….40

About Ahmard………………………..41

Notes……....…………………………….43

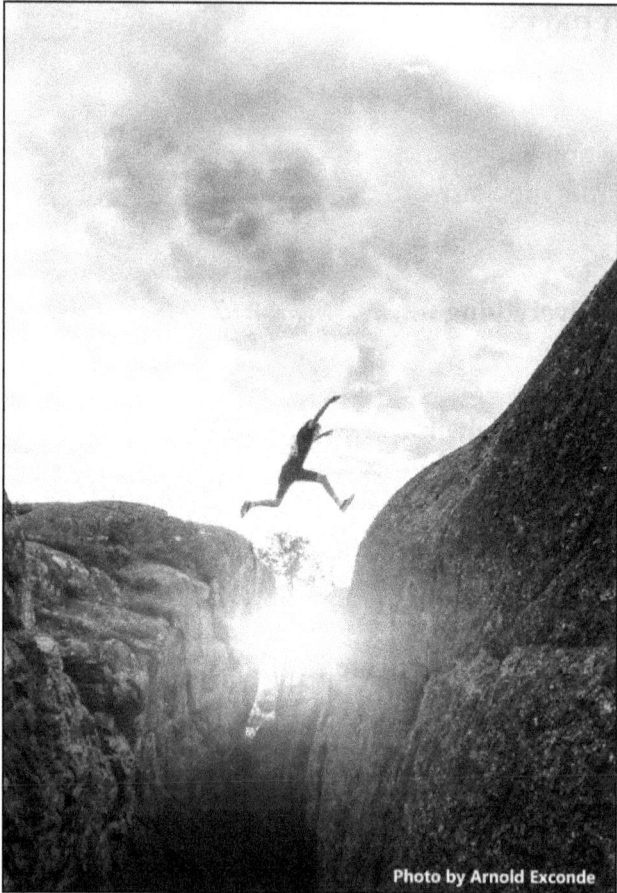

Photo by Arnold Exconde

Proudly Say...

I Am More Than Enough...

INTRODUCTION
Good From the Start

How often do we find ourselves asking questions and frantically seeking answers? You don't have to answer that that; however, I'm sure the answer is…a lot.

By all means, continue asking questions. As we all seek to improve on this journey called life, it is important to remember that knowledge and wisdom can be gained on a day-by-day basis. There are so many instances that provide insight when the awareness meter is turned on and fully functioning. No matter what your current status is emotionally, financially, professionally, spiritually, or relationally, you are good – or perhaps even great – right where you stand.

Oh, I know some of you are reading this and saying, "You have no idea what I'm going through. If you knew my story…" And with that, you are correct. I don't know. I do, however, know that whatever the circumstance, it is not greater than the power within you. That power is unlimited, and always available. But, I also admit that it took me a while to realize that.

It took one of the most challenging moments in my adult life before I realized the lesson that I was Good From the Start. It all began the night after my 33rd birthday when my mother left 5 frantic messages on my voicemail.

BACKGROUND

My entire life, my father was the example of many things for me. The father I am referring to is my step-father. I would rather not recognize that title because he chose to be my father when he married my mother. I simply say I was blessed to have two fathers.

Where I felt my father's most valuable impact was in my late 20s and early 30s, when I needed to deal with issues where my moral compass was tested. My challenges were the usual ones in that transition between being a teenager and being an adult, when the difference between what is right and what is ethically right isn't always obvious. On many occasions, I called my father when tough morality decisions had to be made. No matter what he had going on, he made it a priority to share his wisdom. Most of the time, his advice turned out to be advantageous to all parties involved. I must admit that I became dependent on his wisdom for so many decisions.

In November 2011, all of that came to an end when I got that phone message from my mother. "Your father is dying." I didn't want to believe it.

THE REQUEST

Prior to arriving at the hospital, I made a simple request of God. "I just want my father to walk out of this hospital." That's all. Simple and to the point. I said, "I know that you are all powerful and can make that happen. Please, please, answer this prayer."

Sadly, my mother was right and my father died. The night after my 33rd birthday. Out of nowhere. No warning. No goodbye. It literally went from "I'm coming by to show you my newly-published book and crack a cold one with you," to "I can't believe this is happening. He's really gone?"

I needed to console my family, but I was pissed off at God for ignoring the most important prayer of my life. I stepped outside of the hospital, overtaken by anger. I had to ask a few questions...

- How did we get here?

- What now am I supposed to do?

I realized that I was not prepared for this moment. Or was I?

THE STRUGGLE

Here's the dilemma I faced in those first minutes after my father's death. How was I supposed to be the person he had been teaching me to be?

He taught me how to check my moral compass, live a life of integrity and was the example of how to treat everyone with respect, regardless of how they treated me. Had I mastered the lessons he had taught me enough for me to even graduate? My knee-jerk answer was, "No."

My confidence level had never been lower than in those first distraught moments. Somehow, I turned within, and engaged in an inner dialogue with God in a way I had never done before.

The questions I asked were...

- How is this seemingly tragic event a great moment for me?

- What do you want me to think in this moment?

- What lesson am I to learn from this?

And then, I heard that still angelic voice speak to me..."Your dad has given you all you need to succeed and survive. In fact, you have always had this within you."

Me: "I only asked you for one thing God, to make sure that my father walks out of this hospital. Only one thing. Did you not hear me?"

God: "My son, I have honored your request. You asked for your father to walk out of the hospital. He is, through you. You embody all that he stood for. Now, go out into the world and let your light shine. You were always Good From the Start."

Oh. My. God. My face was wet with my tears and sweat. I felt as though hours had passed; however, it had been mere minutes. I thought, "Wow you mean to tell me that I've been walking the earth for over 30 years and I learned more about myself in the last eight minutes than in the previous 30 years?" Could this be true? I've been Good From the Start all along?

This is what I heard. This is what I've come to believe.

LESSONS FROM MY FATHER

BELIEF – The qualities you seek to live a better life are already within you. You will have to cultivate those traits and continue to practice forming new habits. However, realize that potential is already there. It's a mindset that will require a great deal of work, and it all starts with the belief that you lack nothing.

Imagine your early childhood days. You know, before words like "can't" entered your vocabulary, and long before doubt was even an issue in your life. If you are anything like my siblings and I, we played make believe. If you were like me, the characters you played were always the biggest and baddest people who existed, real or imagined. It didn't matter. If you believed with that radical imagination, it was true. Failure was not an option. And what was so awesome about this is that no one could tell us otherwise. Out-of-this-world, out-of-the-box thinking propelled us each day. The question is what happened? Or better yet, what changed?

TAKE ACTION – Belief is the kick start for taking action. If you want something and believe in it, then you cannot help but to take action. When you affirm that *I Am More Than Enough*, the action is empowered and fueled by this mindset.

Knowing that *I Am More Than Enough* helps build the confidence that the actions you take are the ones needed to achieve the outcome you want. You can know that you have not jumped in too fast. You can have the assurance that you are in the flow and that the actions that follow are exactly the ones needed at that time.

One aspect of taking action is to know that you can. Be aware of your self talk. Knowing that you are *More Than Enough* helps keep doubts and fear of failure at bay.

ENDURANCE – I'm a fortunate man because I have had two fathers in my life. My biological father is still here, and he has often said to me, "Son you have to pay your dues." This is a reminder that success is achieved step by step, not all at once.

In 2011, I first identified this idea that *I Am More Than Enough*, but that doesn't mean that I've fully gotten it. I have to repeat this affirmation every day in much the same way that exercise must be repeated consistently to remain fit. *I Am More Than Enough* is like a favorite song on repeat throughout the day, every day.

We hear all the time, Life is a marathon, not a sprint. The same goes for an empowered mind. You play this for the long haul, consistently reinforcing the *I Am More Than Enough* attitude.

AND FINALLY

If you are anything like me, you may have wandered through life, seeking what you think you lack. Well, your search over. In the pages ahead, you will learn that the opinion you have of you is the only one that matters and the practice of self love and forgiveness is the greatest gifts to give to yourself. All that is asked of you is to be willing to initiate and accept your inevitable growth. The principles presented will reinforce the truth that you are *More Than Enough*.

It's not a bad thing to rediscover you. Sometimes you have to reintroduce yourself, to yourself. As William Shakespeare said, "To thine own self be true." Only you know what it takes to do you. Make that happen. You are the only you there is. Get real with you knowing that the truth lies within. And know that the power within is all that there really is, and it's all you need to know that you are *More Than Enough*.

Now, go be that.

Chapter 1
Image is Everything

"Loving the person you see in the mirror each morning is the foundation to an empowered life."

Maxwell Maltz, creator of Psycho-Cybernetics, said, "The opinion you have of yourself is the only one that matters." So the question is this: how do you develop a healthy opinion of yourself? It all begins with self-image, and how much you value and love yourself.

To be honest, it's time to be selfish...or better yet, self serving. Many in society frown at the idea of this because mostly this is seen as negative. In the example though, it is absolutely necessary to use this.

Image is Everything is the first of three points, which focuses on having a healthy self image. This is where the self serving comes in. Meaning your primary attention as it pertains to self improvement begins with your own mental attitude. How do you view yourself currently?

Do you see yourself as a success, a failure, a survivor, or are you contempt with just being an okay person? Be honest with yourself here as this is the groundwork needed to recognize the successes and shortcomings in every area of your life.

SELFIE EXERCISE

Pull out your cell phone and take a selfie. If you don't have the capability to take one, go look in the mirror. Now examine yourself.

What qualities of character do you see? Write down "I AM" followed by 7 words to describe yourself. Stay away from hygienic things like hair style, shaving and blemishes. After you have written your list, notice how many of them are positive and empowering. Notice the ones that are not.
You now have the basis to identify the aspects of your self-image that you may want to transform, from the inside out.

Remember! I Am is a proclamation about yourself. Self-image is a major aspect of that. If you identified any aspect of character that makes you feel disempowered or inadequate, imagine how to rewrite that quality to its opposite. For example, if you wrote failure, what is its opposite for you? Successful is the obvious opposite, but if you don't believe that you are, then proclaiming, "I Am Successful" may feel like a lie. You can always begin with *I Am More Than Enough* to become whatever you desire.

A daily practice to begin changing your self-image to one that empowers you is to say to yourself, when you awaken, "*I Am More Than Enough.*" Write this down and tape it to the mirror in your bathroom or vanity so it becomes part of your morning ritual in getting ready for the day. Repeat this to yourself throughout the day as you encounter life's unexpected roadblocks. In addition to the reciting of this power-affirming affirmation, here are three ways that will enhance your self image.

SELF FORGIVENESS

Are you hanging onto any regrets, large or small? The truth is that everyone makes mistakes. Sometimes people wallow in the consequences of a mistake for weeks to years. This feels terrible, right? This mistake grows in your mind and becomes a burden. Instead, own what happened, deal with the consequences, identify what you learned and vow to be better the next time. And here's the most important part. Forgive yourself. If you could have done better at the time you made the mistake, you would have.

SELF-FORGIVENESS EXERCISE

Identify a mistake that you've made that has become a burden to you because you haven't let it go. Write it down with as much detail as you need to feel that you have fully described this thing that makes you feel badly. Give the mistake a title.

Now, affirm: I Am willing to forgive myself for MISTAKE TITLE and for its consequences.

Repeat this affirmation every day for 28 days, by which time release has probably come to you.

Remember I Am? Holding on to negative thoughts about yourself is a proclamation that can produce only more negativity. Before long, that bitterness starts to creep into other actions you engage in. The inevitable result is anger and resentment towards yourself that you may take out on others. This is an example of the thoughtless misuse of I Am that can occur when you fail to forgive yourself.

EMBRACE A NEW DAY

As you forgive and release the harsh feelings towards yourself, you undoubtedly feel refreshed. Now you have a clean slate. There are no do-overs and tomorrow is always just beyond your grasp. All we ever have is the present.

The present. Treat it like a gift to yourself because it is. Live life to the fullest. You can't embrace all the good that life brings if you are still bothered over past mistakes. Start anew with an intention of living in the current life experience, working to make it better than some decisions of the past.

When you live in the present, you are empowered because you're not distracted by past mistakes. Instead, you are focused on what the most important thing to do right now is as you respect time and act with a sense of urgency. Remember in all of these moments you are *More Than Enough,* meaning you can transcend every moment and recreate the life experience you desire.

WHAT'S GOOD HERE?

About three years ago, I was going through one personal crisis after another.

My marital relationship was falling apart, which led to separation and eventual divorce. My income plunged by 60 percent after losing my national media gig. My puppy of nine years had an inoperable tumor that led to her death. And on top of all of that I was at odds with a few of my family members due to my bad choices and misguided priorities.

Every day, I was weighed down by anger, depression and, eventually, anxiety. I kept finding reasons to be mad at myself, my situations and even God. What did I do to deserve all of this? Why was everyone and everything against me? As you can see, I had quite the pity party.

After a long, unhealthy stretch of all these unproductive emotions, I wondered what advice my deceased father would have had for me. The answer came to me in the form of a question: "Is there anything good here within all of this mess?"

I discovered there was a lot of good that I had simply been ignoring during that year and a half. Necessity required I get out of the comfort zone of my home office, which I no longer had. Losing more than half of my income required me to look differently at how I earned a living. I also decided to double the amount of community service projects. Somehow, I always managed to have enough in my account to cover my monthly expenses even though some months ended with a mere $8.27 left as a remaining balance. This difficult period ended up being one of the happiest of my adult life.

An epiphany happened: I doubled up on the service rendered, decided to give more of myself and, ultimately, I became more. That became my new focus on life. So, how did I begin?

On a sheet of paper, I wrote two columns. The left one identified the problem, and the right one identified either something directly good about the problem or something positive that had flowed from the problem.

WHAT'S GOOD HERE? EXERCISE

The Problem	What's Good?

You can do this self-assessment, which allows you to see how adversity results in growth. If you are like me, you want growth to come when things are going well. Sadly, that does not seem to be how it works.

Set aside some time to be quiet with yourself. Meditate (which will be discussed in Chapter 3). Then write your own "What's Good Here" list to identify the adversity you are currently facing.

Have you ever noticed how focused you become on the small blessings of life after something that's convenient gets taken from you? The things you take for granted suddenly becomes something you pay close attention to. You see this a lot during natural disasters, and I had my own experience with this not long after I finished college. For me, that small blessing turned out to be a cup of ice.

In 2005, close to 1 million residents were encouraged to evacuate Houston to get out of the path of Hurricane Rita. I evacuated with a fraternity brother to Nacogdoches, Texas, the city where I had gone to college. The plan was to stay at the fraternity house where we had lived while in school. The bumper-to-bumper traffic turned the normally 90-minute drive into 14 hours during a day of extreme heat. Once in Nacogdoches, the hits kept coming. The power went out so we had to use an outdoor grill to barbeque all of the food in the refrigerator. We had plenty of food, water and Gatorade, but no ice.

The one store where we could get ice was across the street from the university, near the fraternity house. The line to get ice was about 2.5 hours long, and to ensure there would be enough ice to distribute, only one 64-ounce cup per person was allowed. When my friend came home from the store, he poured some Gatorade over that ice. One by one each of us, about 12 of us total, took turns taking a sip from the cup. It was a moment of sacred, appreciative communion where everyone shared so enough was there for us all to be refreshed.

After taking that drink, everyone became much more calm and relaxed. So in the midst of no power, a natural disaster, this small serving of ice shared among us was something to be grateful for. More than a decade has passed since then, and each time I remember this I'm even more grateful than I was in the moment.

Adversity can indeed bring out the best in you when you choose to push past the situation and look for the advantages within everything. Remember you are the common denominator in every moment, so having healthy self image will place you in a winning mindset more times than not. The time is now to grow in the midst of life's challenges, no matter good, bad or indifferent.

A healthy self image gives you the confidence to see life's moments as opportunities to think and grow. Operate from the potential that you are *More Than Enough*.

You live from the inside out, therefore the outer conditions never dictate your belief in you, unless you allow it to. And why would you ever want that? It doesn't care about you as much as you do.

Chew on that for a moment before moving on to the next point.

AFFIRMATION

When I awaken this morning, I am a winner. I am beautiful and capable of achieving everything I want as I show up as the best version of me. I believe this and I am this.

Chapter 2
Accepting Yourself

"The real truth exists in your mind, which creates the reality by which you live. It becomes your personal commandment."

What have you said to you, about you?

We previously explored Image is Everything and that self-talk is a vital part of developing an unshakeable self-image. The next principle is Accepting Yourself. Image is about how you see yourself. Accepting Yourself is about embracing and valuing the qualities that make you unique. The language you use to describe yourself on a daily basis reveals the truth of how accepting of yourself that you are.

Do you constantly put a magnifying glass on your shortcomings? Do you tell yourself you are anything but a capable winner? Words have power, plenty of power. What you tell yourself consistently over time ends up becoming your life experience, which ends up being who you are. You may have heard it said, "we become what we think about," a statement made famous by Earl Nightingale. If you discover this is true, the question is this: What do you want to be true about you?

You were born lacking nothing at all. Everything you could ever want or need is already within. From inception, you were created in love and born with infinite possibilities, no matter who your biological parents are or your family history. You have life experiences, talents and a way of seeing the world that no one else in the world has had.

As we explored in the chapter Image is Everything, positive self talk is one effective tool to set the tone in building your self image and creating the foundation for your authentic self. However, that image will not stick if you do not accept yourself, or if you choose to compare yourself to some false ideal or to other people.

Age old wisdom states, "out of the heart, the mouth speaks." Remember, the heart is the feeling nature of your thoughts. The mind thinks, the heart feels and the mouth speaks. These are the powerful steps that create your truth. Everything begins with thought, then you speak, followed by you hearing and feeling your thoughts articulated. This is how your thoughts come full circle. Your words have meaning and power. Now a decision must be made. Does the mind accept what has been said, or reject it? When your heart speaks truth about yourself through your mouth, what is the truth you are saying about yourself? I once had a mentor who used to tell me that the mind does not take jokes. The point here is to be careful with the words that come out of your mouth. Henry Ford, the founder of the Ford Motor Company said, "whether you think you can or you think you can't, you're right."

When that spoken thought comes back to your mind, and it is accepted, it's now a building block towards your personal truth of how you see yourself and of how accepting of yourself that you are. Self-acceptance begins with being willing to see yourself with the same level of compassion that you would extend to a good friend by encouraging them to appreciate their own talents and skills.

BEWARE OF "GOOD" AND "BAD" LABELS

Have you ever noticed how descriptive people get when relating their worst life challenges? Conversely, when a seemingly great experience occurs, the details are simple and lack explanation? Why is that?

One reason is that labels are placed on every incident, mainly as good or bad occurrences. As you build up your self-acceptance account, placing rigid labels on different life events mirrors the judgment already in place. A shift in perspective is needed to better understand that challenges typically bring your greatest opportunity for growth. Occurrences categorized as good may only be temporary. Those labeled as bad may turn out to be the most valuable over time. If you can simply accept the moment for what it is, the answers you seek will come to you.

LABEL EXERCISE

Imagine a challenging event that has caused you ongoing pain. What is the story that you are telling yourself about that event. Now, imagine that event as a blessing in your life. What is the new story you might tell about that event? Then consider whether you would be growing into the person you are today if that event had not happen.

When viewed in this new perspective, life's challenges may no longer carry the negative messages they once did – all because you changed your perspective about what the event meant.

THE POWER OF "NO"

A minister friend recently told me these words, "No is a complete sentence."

At the time, I was worried about how I was going to overcome obstacles that made me feel overwhelmed. I had accepted too many gigs out of a sense of obligation and had made demanding unrealistic expectations of myself to the point that I was not functioning. I had forgotten that I had the choice to say, no. When I did, I immediately felt a sense of relief and renewed optimism.

Are you one of those people who has difficulty saying, no, and then feels guilty if you do? Or do you feel overwhelmed, overworked, underappreciated and undervalued when you feel pressured to say yes? A huge aspect of self-acceptance is to be willing to say no. When you do, you are making room for yourself, based on your standards.

To empower your life, know what you want and be willing to set aside time and space for that want, whatever it may be. Then, be willing to defend it by telling others no when they want to encroach on it. For example, let's say that you and your family have scheduled family fun Friday nights. This means that you can say "no" when a close friend asks you to join him and other guys for happy hour on Friday night. Maybe you want to take a class, learn to paint, want an hour to read to your children, or something else that somehow has a perceived (by others) low priority, even though you feel fulfilled and happy when you do it. Shouldn't these be high priority items? Be willing to say "no" to the requests that keep you from putting yourself and your interests first.

Stop focusing on pleasing others and start with what makes you happy and satisfied. After you start to implement this principle in other areas of your life, it sets the standard. When you stand up for yourself by speaking boldly on the boundaries you set, it puts everyone on notice that you value yourself enough to claim the way you want to live your life and the intended results you desire.

SAYING NO EXERCISE

Methods to say no without insulting others include things like:

• Thank the person for thinking of you. You've been asked because you are trusted.

• Say "no" to the request, which is different than saying "no" as a rejection of the person. When appropriate, offer an alternative.

• Accept that sometimes you are going to miss out. Your level of regret about missing out will be a good cue for you in the exercise of your "no" muscle and recognizing the instances where you may prefer "yes."

• Practice. Like any skill, this gets easier with practice. For inspiration, notice a toddler who is learning to say "no." This desire is born out of self-autonomy, which everyone needs to learn ...and sometimes relearn.

If you label yourself as a people pleaser, you may be tempted to say "yes" to the obligations that others bring to you at work and at home. Take notice of all the times you have said "yes" to things that others regard as urgent or important but have little to do with your priorities.

When one of these comes up, have the courage to say "no." This is a beginning step to manage the expectations of others and to affirm that your priorities are important.

JUDGE NOT
You can be your own worst enemy.

In your quest for greatness, you need to set goals and have high aspirations. However, be careful to avoid unrealistic expectations that lead to putting extreme pressure on yourself. You already know what extreme pressure leads to – feeling overwhelmed and judgmental of yourself.

When you begin a project that is unfamiliar and new, you probably research or consult someone who has the knowledge, strategies and skills to assist. Then you proceed despite still being unsure of the end result. If it doesn't work out the first time, how do you react? Do you label the effort as a failure? Or do you label the effort as part of the learning curve? One of these judgments serves you, and the other does not.

LETTING GO OF JUDGMENT EXERCISE

To remove a debilitating mindset from your experience, begin making a mental shift by reminding yourself that you are *More Than Enough*. Thomas Edison famously asserted that he didn't fail a thousand times in creating a light bulb; instead, he took a thousand steps. He knew that he was *More Than Enough*. Michael Jordan was labeled as an ordinary basketball player when he was in high school, and the low expectations others had for him did not match his huge vision for himself. Instead of giving in, he knew that he was *More Than Enough*; secure in this, he practiced and became a legend.

Have the courage to say to yourself, "I love me as I am. And *I Am More Enough*."

Love yourself through the process. Love yourself through all of life's ups and downs. Trust that you will be just fine in the long run.

SELF (LOVE) IMPROVEMENT
Many spiritual teachers and philosophers have said, "change your thinking to change your life." Many of these same

philosophers have also taught that "what you resist persists." Both of these ideas suggest that if you want to improve yourself in any capacity, it helps to start by first loving the current version of you, regardless of how far you may appear to be from your intended goal.

Accepting yourself means that you acknowledge and appreciate the current state of your affairs, even as you push for self-improvement. Whether the goal is to be more physically fit, obtain a new job, achieve a promotion, enter into a relationship or anything else that you feel will improve your life, this is the moment to suspend any harsh comments and beliefs about yourself.

SELF (LOVE) IMPROVEMENT EXERCISE

Watch a toddler who is learning how to walk. Though she may fall and cry when she does, she doesn't quit. She keeps at it, often with the excited encouragement of the adults around her. Now, imagine this as an experience where every time the child falls, she is criticized, labeled, and berated. This sounds awful, right? Be honest with yourself. Have you criticized, labeled, and berated yourself for a mistake or for being less skilled than you want to be when you embark on something new?

Instead of beating yourself up, say to yourself, "*I Am More Than Enough.*" This kind of encouragement is key to achieving anything you desire.

Do not confuse acceptance with giving up. Acceptance in this context merely means that you acknowledge how things are now, you strive to forgive yourself for any mistaken actions or beliefs that have created the current situation and you embrace your realization that you are *More Than Enough* to make the changes you desire.

Imagine a specific goal that may seem too challenging to achieve. Every time you become aware of your negative judgments about your ability, say to yourself, "*I Am More Than Enough* to be successful." Then act as though the statement is true...because it is.

ACCEPT THE TRUTH OF WHO YOU TRULY ARE

Choose to speak empowerment and positivity into your experience, especially when the experiences you are having do not match what you prefer. These four practices (being aware of labels, saying no, letting go of negative judgments and practicing self-love) help you to fulfill your goals and to avoid beating yourself up when challenges arise.

Maintaining a positive mindset can be difficult in this era in which more information is shared than any time in human history. The attention-grabbing information is often fear-based. Though being informed is important, you want to ensure that you deflect the fear mongering in favor of positive ideals and optimism. Why?

Remember what so many philosophers teach? Change your thinking, change your life. If that's true, you want to ensure the beliefs you develop and the actions you take are as a result of those beliefs which move you towards your goals rather than towards what you fear. The choice is up to you. What view you have about yourself will become your truth.

Every morning when you awaken, tell yourself, "I was created to be awesome." Now, every morning, will you believe that? Probably not. But, imagine telling yourself the opposite. Such a statement would be disempowering, and it will keep you from building a life that works well. Remember, whatever you consistently tell yourself over time becomes your life reality.

BE PREPARED

The strongest detriment to believing you are *More Than Enough* is fear. It will forever have a place at the table as long as you allow it. You speak wealth; poverty appears to be waiting for you to slip. Speak good health; sickness seems to be on call. Proclaim confidence, and doubt seems ready to step in.

The key is to stay sharp and protect your most valuable asset – your mind. Prepare yourself each day by telling yourself that you are *More Than Enough* to accomplish your goals. Your mind, until instructed otherwise, will take as the truth the words you have given it. Help it along by giving it positive thoughts spoken as affirmations. Stay alert and affirm *"I Am More Than Enough"* at every turn and moment. Imagine how great your life becomes when you begin to know that you are telling yourself the truth.

"I Am More Than Enough" is a gift that will keep on giving every day that you embrace it. Go ahead and open it and enjoy. You deserve it.

AFFIRMATION

On this day, I accept me, as me. I love who I am which is *More Than Enough.*

Chapter 3
Mindful Changes

"Be proactive and initiate your transformation. Otherwise, changes that happen outside of you may not be beneficial for the life experience you expect."

In the previous chapters, you began the process of affecting positive change in your life by absorbing the principles behind Image is Everything and Accepting Yourself.

Change is constant. Change is life, as any cycle of seasons demonstrates. Nature also shows a predictable change is good. What about those instances of unexpected change? Are you still judging them as good or bad? Or, are you seeing them as opportunities?

Within you there is already power to affect positive change in your life. You have the ability to adapt to any change that may come your way. Here's an idea, since you know that change is constant, why not embrace it? Even more, why not develop the skills that will help you overcome the unexpected and become the architect for the changes you want?

Though things often turn out differently that you may plan for, you are more likely to have changes you prefer when you stand firm on the idea that you are mentally equipped for what may come your way. Knowing you are mentally equipped is first a choice of deciding that you are, practicing the skills on a consistent basis and keeping your focus on the important tasks.

JUST DECIDE

How often have you heard people say that they want to do something new yet they have trouble figuring this out? It's true that the decision process is not one that comes easily. Go ahead and ask yourself, "What is it that I really want?"

If you are like me, you may have trouble giving a precise answer to so simple a question. Chances are that an answer will not come to you immediately. In fact, it may not happen within minutes, hours, or even days. The issue is a lack of clarity, which is often the result of too much noise going on all around us with our work, family, television and constant social media updates via our phones.

In the technological times we live in, distractions are common. To gain the clarity, you need to limit these distractions. The first step to gain clarity is to meditate, which helps calm the mind and gain focus. To expand on this simple meditation, add a word that focuses your mind on something you want, such as calm, love, peace or some other word (a single syllable works best) that is meaningful to you.

Another addition to this practice is to have in mind a question that you would like an answer to when you begin meditation. Write down the question. Then let go of the question while you meditate. When you finish meditating, write down any thoughts or insights that come to you. Do not over think this. When you come out of meditation and nothing comes to mind but a clear head that is okay. There are right or wrongs with this practice.

SIMPLE MEDITATION EXERCISE

You can find hundreds of meditation techniques in books, audio recordings and online. A simple way to begin a meditation practice is this one: Focus on the breath.

- Go to a quiet place – preferably in your home– and tune out as much outside noise as possible. Sit comfortably.

- Close your eyes and take a couple of deep breaths. Inhale for a four-second count and then exhale. Do this five times and then sit still.

After taking in the breaths, remain in stillness. The objective here is taking your mind off everything. Simply be in the moment. Take in another breath. To encourage your mind to become quiet, say softly to yourself, "Breathe" as you release the breath. Repeat this for five minutes. If you cannot do five minutes, begin with a minute, then work up to three minutes, five minutes and eventually to fifteen minutes.

Try making this simple meditation a daily practice. Many people find this a great way to begin their day.

To gain the clarity needed to make changes, this practice is one of the best. It opens the mind so that it is ready to receive new insights and directions. When this becomes a continual practice, you will likely have an enhanced level of awareness. With heightened awareness, you will be mentally prepared to make new and empowered choices and have the confidence needed to pursue those choices.

After you have clarity about what you want, then visualizing the change you would like to experience is possible. Think of it like this, if your mind is the canvas, meditation clears all the previous images. Visualization, or creative imagination, allows you paint a new work of art. These are the mental pictures that create the life you want to experience.

VISUALIZATION EXERCISE

Begin with a simple meditation that focuses on the breath, but this time, allow yourself to imagine freely and without judgments of any kind (good or bad). How would the idea look, be and feel. Allow yourself up to fifteen minutes for the visualization.

Then, write down in as much detail as is meaningful to you how this would be. Don't judge anything about this. The sky is the limit. Anything is possible.

You have just given your imagination a powerful boost, and after you finish, your mind will likely be playing with the ideas you have given it. Some of these may be concrete plans and goals that you want to write down. Some of these may be expansions on the original visualization.

If you have the idea that the simple visualization exercise has a halo effect that may last for days or weeks, you would be correct.

DO WHAT'S MOST IMPORTANT
"The main thing is to keep the main thing the main thing."

Those are the wise words of Stephen Covey from his book *The 7 Habits of Highly Effective People*. After you decide to make a change that is clear and you have concretely placed in your mind, you are able to plan and prioritize. Simply put, do what's most important first.

Imagine that you decide to launch that business you've dreamed of. You are excited and ready to start. A project of this size clearly has many steps. Those steps suggest there is some order in which this will unfold that might include research and funding, finding a location to set up shop, obtaining needed materials, advertising your product or service, hiring people and so on. You may be faced with deciding what the most important thing is right now. Here's the beauty of the process you just went through with meditation and developing clarity. This can be used for the big picture of your life, and it can be used for the finite aspects of your life, both in business and in your personal life. Warren Buffet has reduced this to a three-step process with his advice of, "Know what you want. Learn the tools to get your there. Have insane focus to combine the first two."

Deciding the most important thing to do right now comes out of what you value most in life. A colleague, Dr. John Demartini, has done extensive research on what drives human behavior. He states that every human being lives and operates from a set of values. What a person values most requires little to no outside motivation for its fulfillment, no matter how mundane the current task. You can see this at work in your own life. If you do not highly value whatever is before you, each task requires continual outside motivation for the completion of the task.

UNEXPECTED CHANGE HAPPENS
You have probably been in the same position I have where you're progressing well on your goals and an unexpected, sometimes catastrophic change crashes down on you. It could be the loss of a job or an accident or a death in the family or a natural disaster. Here is what I have come to know and believe with all my heart: whatever you are faced with, you have what it takes to overcome this.

The processes described in this chapter (meditating, getting clear about what you want, and doing the most important thing now) are the same ones you can use to get through the unwanted, unexpected change that is thrust upon you. That five minute meditation to become calm and clear is still available. Above all, maintain that certain knowledge that, "*I Am More Than Enough*" to get through this situation.

STAYING FRESH

Sometimes I get bored and frustrated with my progress. If you are like me, this has happened to you. The following are suggestions that may help you from becoming stagnant, which can happen even within actions that produce optimal results.

"You're only as good as yesterday's results." This can serve as a reminder that today is a new day, and it's time to create anew. See now the change is being initiated by you from you with the intention of generating new experiences. This will completely transform your life because now you are being proactive instead of reactive.

Add variety to your daily rituals. I know a man who drinks from a different coffee mug each morning. In addition to this, for one month, he ate at a different restaurant each day for lunch, deliberately choosing unfamiliar places. This may seem weird to you, but you'll be surprised how much of your life is on autopilot. And while some habits are great and should continue, allowing the mind to experience new things is imperative.

Your practice of this might be to take a different route home or park somewhere different. These small, yet mindful changes help you more than you know. In short, add some small adjustments to your daily routine to offer variety and to help keep your mind stimulated.

The most important part of staying fresh is the reminder that you are being deliberate and mindful as you go through your life rather than falling into habits that become so much a routine that life becomes one of stagnation.

AFFIRMATION

In this moment, I choose to be an active participant in my life. I will not sit around and allow life to dictate my terms. I've been given the gift of life. It's time to live it.

Chapter 4
I AM-Ness: Time to Activate

"You only have two personalities that require your undivided attention: your authentic self (the I AM self) and your ego. Control the latter and you will make huge strides in improving yourself."

Let's focus on two words that are key to defining yourself and your total life experience: I AM.

Image is Everything

Accepting Yourself

Mindful Changes

These three ideas are core to power that I AM provides, which is a solid frame for becoming your best self, being truthful with yourself and others and accepting that change is inevitable.

Self talk usually begins with I AM. What follows those two words? Affirmation? Criticism? The words, I AM, are a statement of truth. I AM" has the power to create, and by that very nature should be used mindfully. While it can create and build your self image, it may also be the source of negative emotions.

33

When you embrace the power of I AM, it's a foreshadowing of what's to come. Think about this, there are times when what you proclaim may not be what you truly feel. But the power of affirmative words is key in personal development. Christian Music Group Hillsong Worship has an empowering song with lyrics that addresses this very notion:

Let the weak say, "I am strong"
Let the poor say, "I am rich"

So when you feel one emotion, proclaim its positive and empowering opposite.

I AM tired – I AM energetic

I AM discouraged – I AM inspired

I AM worried – I AM confident

I AM faint – I AM powerful

I AM is the ultimate affirmation. To say I AM is to proclaim the truth about who you are and the power you possess within.

I AM can be hitched to positive or negative statements. And since I AM is a declaration of truth, what you choose for you becomes your own personal truth and law.

The recognition of I AM is powerful and advantageous, but can also be a detriment if you misuse it deliberately or thoughtlessly out of habit.

I AM EXERCISE

Each morning awaken with the intention to embrace an attitude of gratitude.

When you step out of bed…

1. As each foot hits the floor say to yourself, Thank You. This is telling your mind that you are grateful first thing in the morning.

2. With each step, proclaim an I AM affirmation. Do this for 7-10 steps as you walk to your bathroom, kitchen or wherever the first place you go when leaving your bed.

I AM Beautiful. I AM Capable. I AM Intelligent. I AM Worthy. I AM Loved. *I AM More Than Enough.*

Choose to be aware of this great and divine power that is already *More Than Enough*. When you say to yourself, *I Am More Than Enough*, you are affirming that you lack nothing. Instead you are capable and abundant success in every area of your life is attainable. I AM is the definition of your true essence. Use it to create the life experience you want, and deserve.

AFFIRMATION

On this day, look in the mirror and say, "I AM the thinker who thinks the thought who creates the thing*. Therefore, I AM all I need to be great."

* Arthur J. Johnson at the Transformation Experience

LISTEN...

To the quiet voice within

To that subtle knock at the door of opportunity

To the winds of change telling me it's okay

To the "I Love You" whisper I yearn for

To the divine rooster's song of passion that awakens me in
morning

To the footsteps of God carrying me to my divine purpose

To the birds harmonizing the tune *I Am More Than Enough*

To the pleading of my soul to love everyone

To the cries of the speechless souls praying to be heard

To the slow beats of my heart seeking to express compassion

To the boldness of my free will to make empowered choices

To the ocean waves crashing into my to-do list, urging me to live
in the moment

To the beautiful paintings revealing snapshots of my best life

To the throbbing headache telling me it's time to expand my mind

To the tapping on the shoulder as God suggests a new course of action

To the yearning of my future self asking me to join it

To the tingle running down my spine to inform me a breakthrough is coming

To God...To Myself

To the truth that God and I are ONE,

Breathing in the same air...

Exhaling infinite love

Photo by Tyler Lastovich

In Case You Forgot, Say Again...

I Am More Than Enough.

The Finale...

So now you have everything needed to know that you are *More Than Enough*.

Image is Everything – the opinion you have of yourself is the only one that matters

Accepting Yourself – loving who you are as you are is the foundation for self-improvement

Mindful Changes – a focused mind will empower you to be productive when inevitable changes happen in life.

For each principle above, think about an action step you want to begin today. Write it down below to remind yourself:

_____

_____

_____

_____

_____

_____

_____

_____

_____

_____

CONTACT

Book Ahmard today to empower, inspire and motivate your company, team, organization or group.

Bookings/Media Appearance: info@ahmard.com

For program details and to fill out our Pre-Event Questionnaire, visit: www.ahmardvital.com

Call our office at 832-577-1911

@ahmardvital

@ahmardvital

**Follow Ahmard
on Social Media**

Follow Ahmard Vital

Like Ahmard Vital

About The Author

Ahmard Vital, international motivational speaker, entrepreneur, mental performance coach and author, has empowered people globally with his inspirational guidance and tips for self-development. Ahmard provides his audiences with the tools needed to achieve personal success, utilize willpower and determination, and develop strategies that will allow people of all ages to achieve personal and professional excellence. He is adept at empowering athletes, entrepreneurs, business professionals and students with his principles for achievement, which focus on dream building and attaining, goal-setting, and the relentless belief in yourself. By teaching his audiences to recognize their strengths, and capitalize on the power that everyone harnesses within, individuals can realize previously unimagined levels of personal happiness and success.

After nearly a decade of studying the performance habits of high achieving athletes, Ahmard has developed a program of inspiration and motivation that are beneficial to individuals, companies and organizations worldwide.

<u>NOTES</u>

_____

_____

_____

_____

_____

_____

_____

_____

_____

_____

_____

_____

_____

_____

_____

_____

_____

_____

_____

_____

_____

_____

_____

_____

_____

_____

_____

_____

_____

_____

_____

NOTES

NOTES

NOTES

NOTES

NOTES

<u>NOTES</u>

NOTES

NOTES

<u>NOTES</u>

NOTES

NOTES

www.ingramcontent.com/pod-product-compliance
Lightning Source LLC
Chambersburg PA
CBHW060201070426
42447CB00033B/2269